P is for

Inspirational ABC's for Educators

author of NYT Bestseller *Teach Like a Pirate*

Dave Burgess and Shelley Burgess

Illustrated by Genesis M. Kohler

P is for Pirate
© 2014 by Dave Burgess and Shelley Burgess

This book is available at special discounts when purchased in quantity for use as premiums, promotions, fundraising, and educational use. For inquiries and details, contact: daveburgessconsulting@gmail.com.

This publication is designed to provide accurate and authoritative information in regard to the subject matter covered. It is sold with the understanding that the publisher is not engaged in rendering legal, accounting, or other professional service. If legal advice or other expert assistance is required, the services of a competent professional person should be sought.

XEROX® is a registered trademark of Xerox Corporation.
VELCRO® is a registered trademark of Velcro Industries.

Published by Dave Burgess Consulting, Inc.
San Diego, CA
http://daveburgessconsulting.com

Cover and Interior Illustrations by Genesis M. Kohler
Interior Design by My Writers' Connection

Library of Congress Control Number: 2014918691
ISBN Paperback: 978-0-9882176-4-5
ISBN Hard cover: 978-0-9882176-5-2
First Printing: December 2014

DAVE BURGESS
Consulting, Inc.

Discover the Hidden Treasure Within *P is for Pirate!*

What would a book about pirates be without a treasure hunt? Twenty-six pirate-related images are hidden in this book—one per letter. Some are obvious, and some are cleverly disguised. *If* you find all twenty-six images, head to daveburgessconsulting.com and click on the "X" tab (Because, of course, X marks the spot!) to claim your treasure.

"What's the treasure?", you ask. Well, it wouldn't be very pirate-like of us to give away the secret! We know we are biased, but we think you will love it!

Happy hunting!

ACKNOWLEDGMENTS

No good book is ever completed without the awesome support of a first-rate team:

Erin K. Casey (ErinKCasey.com) never ceases to amaze us with her top-notch editing skills and spot-on advice. She continues to serve as a mentor and a friend, and for this project, we are equally grateful to her for connecting us with our fabulous illustrator.

As fans of children's picture books, we know their magic stems from the interactive nature of the words and the pictures on each page. We are indebted to Genesis Kohler for taking our vision, our ideas, and our words and making them come alive in her vivid illustrations that have far exceeded even our best hopes!

As you reach the second half of this book, we know you will enjoy reading the thoughts of more than seventy other smart and connected educators. Each of them is a valuable member of our crew whose thoughts, ideas, and inspiration continue to help us grow.

And finally, our two extraordinary children, Hayden (13) and Ashlyn (11). They don't just put up with our crazy ideas and escapades; they embrace them. Without a doubt, our children are our most precious treasure.

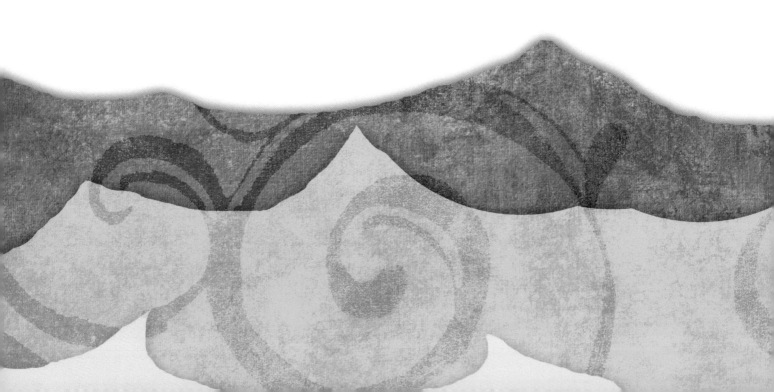

DEDICATION

What a privilege it has been for us to connect with so many amazing educators over the past few years while we have been on this incredible journey. We are truly honored by the reception our work has received and remain eternally grateful for the help you have given us in spreading the *Teach Like a PIRATE* message.

One of the most gratifying parts of the entire voyage has been to see inspirational educators from around the world come together to build the #tlap community and make it a place where passion, creativity, engagement, student empowerment, and support for each other are the order of the day.

Teaching is far more than a profession. It is a calling. To all educators who have embraced this mighty purpose and who venture courageously into classrooms and schools determined to be a powerful, life-changing, world-shaping force for kids, we dedicate this book to you.

With our extreme gratitude,
Dave and Shelley Burgess

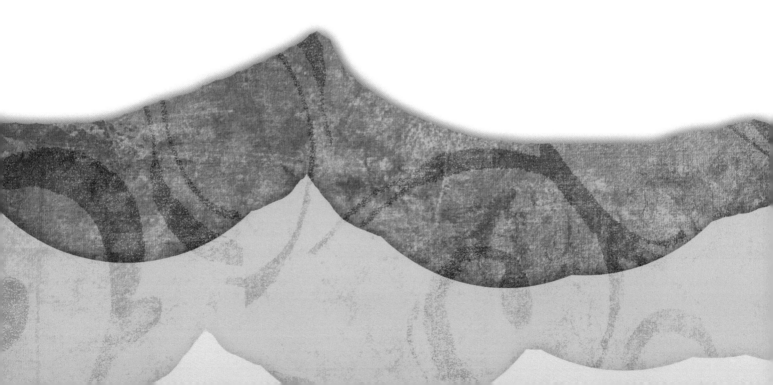

IS FOR

Rough and constantly shifting educational seas make it easy to get thrown off course. Our guiding principles anchor us. We would be hard-pressed to find more secure anchors than these:

> *Every child* can learn.

> *Every child* possesses enormous potential just waiting to be unlocked.

> *Every child* will rise or fall to the level of our expectations.

Empower each student to reach for greatness. Don't settle for anything less.

BUNGEE

is for

"A ship is always safe at the shore, but that is NOT what it is built for."
~Albert Einstein

As educators, sometimes we have to buckle up, conquer our fears, and take a leap of faith. Progress is almost always found outside of our comfort zone. Safe lessons are a recipe for mediocrity.

C is for **CREW**

Savvy pirates don't sail alone; a crew is essential for success. Connecting with educators, building a professional learning network (PLN), and collaborating with a diverse group of mentors, supporters, and peers is critical.

Embrace the synergy of a great team. Surround yourself with people who inspire and challenge you!

#PLNpower

D is for ditch

Ditch that textbook.

Ditch that outdated curriculum.

Ditch those preconceived notions of what is right and wrong in the classroom.

The worst reason to do anything is "because that's the way it has always been done."

E is for elastic

Let's **s t r e t c h** our thinking and empower students to become creators and not just consumers of information. Can they design it, write it, draw it, sculpt it, build it, tweet it, blog it, post it, rap it, sing it, video it, or act it out? Be flexible enough to allow student choice and student voice.

#autonomy
#creativity
#relevancy
#motivation

F is for **FIREWORKS**

Light up the skies of your classroom. Add more **WONDER** and *WOW*—more **BANG** and **BOOM!** Don't just teach a lesson, create an *experience*. Always ask, "How can I make this lesson come alive?" Create a place that kids run to get into instead of run to leave. Make school amazing!

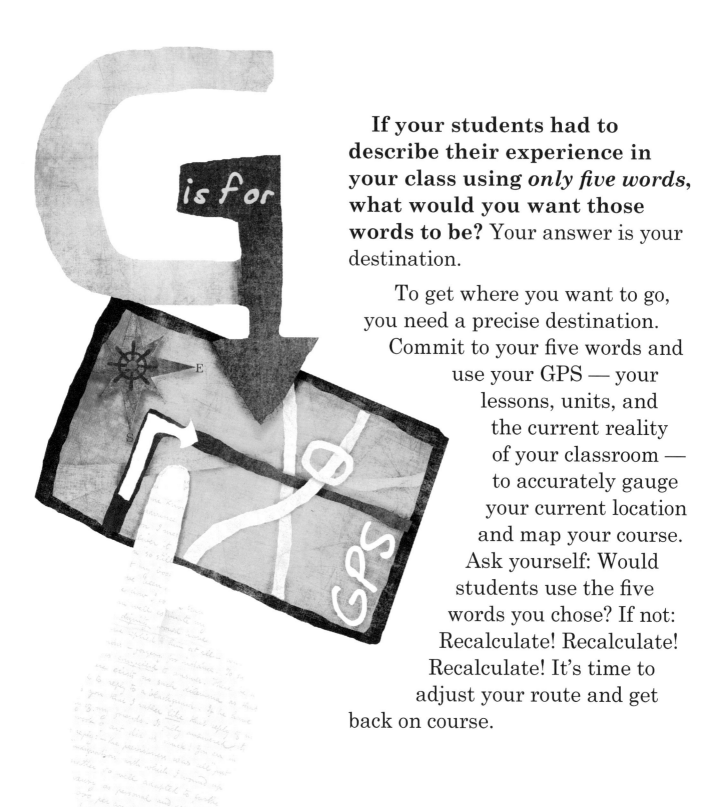

G is for **GPS**

If your students had to describe their experience in your class using _only five words_, what would you want those words to be? Your answer is your destination.

To get where you want to go, you need a precise destination. Commit to your five words and use your GPS — your lessons, units, and the current reality of your classroom — to accurately gauge your current location and map your course. Ask yourself: Would students use the five words you chose? If not: Recalculate! Recalculate! Recalculate! It's time to adjust your route and get back on course.

Every minute counts, even those minutes "around the edges."

Brief interactions during the passing period and breaks—those off-hand remarks and nods in the hallway, those extra-curricular events you attend and clubs you run—**they may make all the difference.**

Each minute spent informally with a student is worth ten hours of class time.

#rapport
#relationships

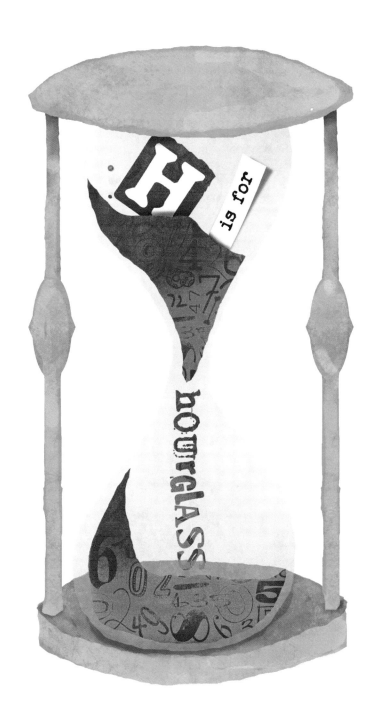

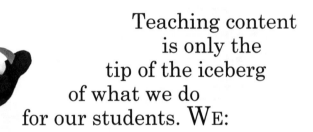

I is for **ICEBERG**

Teaching content
is only the
tip of the iceberg
of what we do
for our students. WE:

BUILD character,

BOOST self-confidence,

KILL apathy,

IGNITE passion,

CULTIVATE creativity,

PROMOTE perseverance, and

FOSTER empathy.

We do so much MORE than what a
test score could possibly reflect...

WE
CHANGE
LIVES.

In jazz we hear a *convergence* of cultures, a *blending* of styles, and a keen emphasis on *improvisation*. The notes on the page provide a starting point, but it's the imaginative and collaborative spirit of the musicians "riffing" off of each other that creates a unique musical experience each time they play. This same spirit fills the best of our schools with the wondrous sounds of learning.

Stir the pot. Cause a commotion. Shake things up!

The status quo in education must change. So, make some noise, ruffle some feathers, and **RAISE A *RUCKUS*.** Sometimes trouble is *worth* starting.

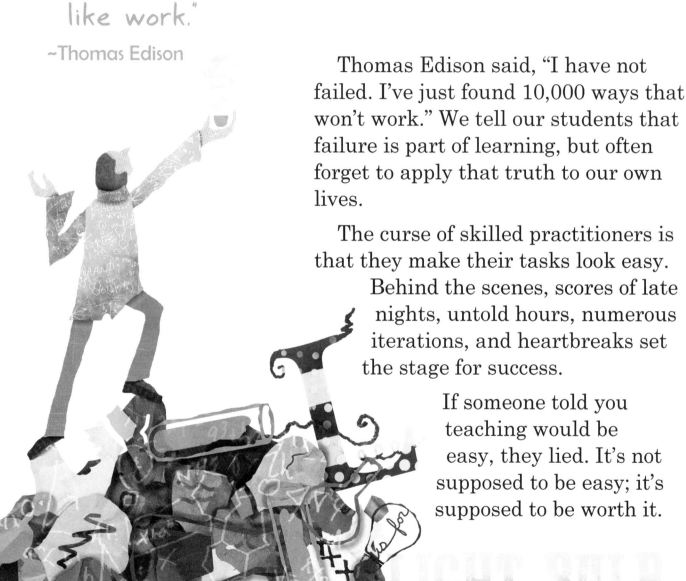

"Most people miss opportunity because it is dressed in overalls and looks like work."

~Thomas Edison

Thomas Edison said, "I have not failed. I've just found 10,000 ways that won't work." We tell our students that failure is part of learning, but often forget to apply that truth to our own lives.

The curse of skilled practitioners is that they make their tasks look easy. Behind the scenes, scores of late nights, untold hours, numerous iterations, and heartbreaks set the stage for success.

If someone told you teaching would be easy, they lied. It's not supposed to be easy; it's supposed to be worth it.

M is for magic

The magic isn't in that latest program or curriculum guide. You won't find it in the standards. It certainly isn't in that next new, bureaucrat-designed initiative.

The magic is in YOU. Often it isn't so much what you do, but rather how you do it. ***You are the magic.***

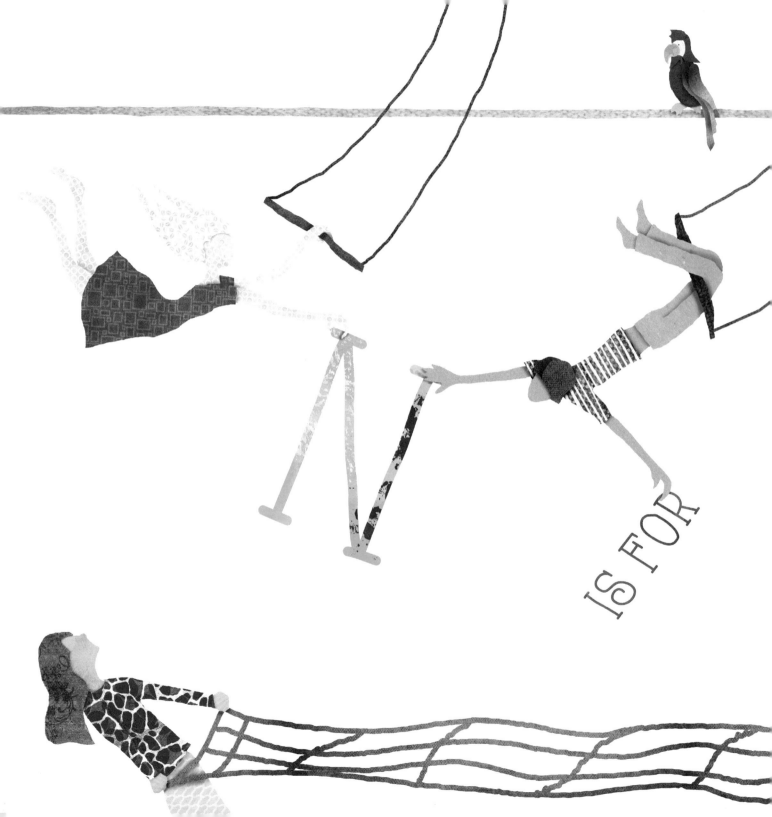

IS FOR

Empower your students to walk the tightrope, swing on the trapeze, and do acrobatics in your classroom. They'll take risks if they know you're there to catch them when they fall.

NET

O is for oxygen

The brain needs oxygen to function best. Designing more opportunities for movement, in and out of the classroom, is a surefire way to increase blood flow, promote health, and provide powerful learning experiences.

Kinesthetic activities help create connections in developing minds and allow students to process information in a whole new way. Let kids jump—*literally*—into learning!

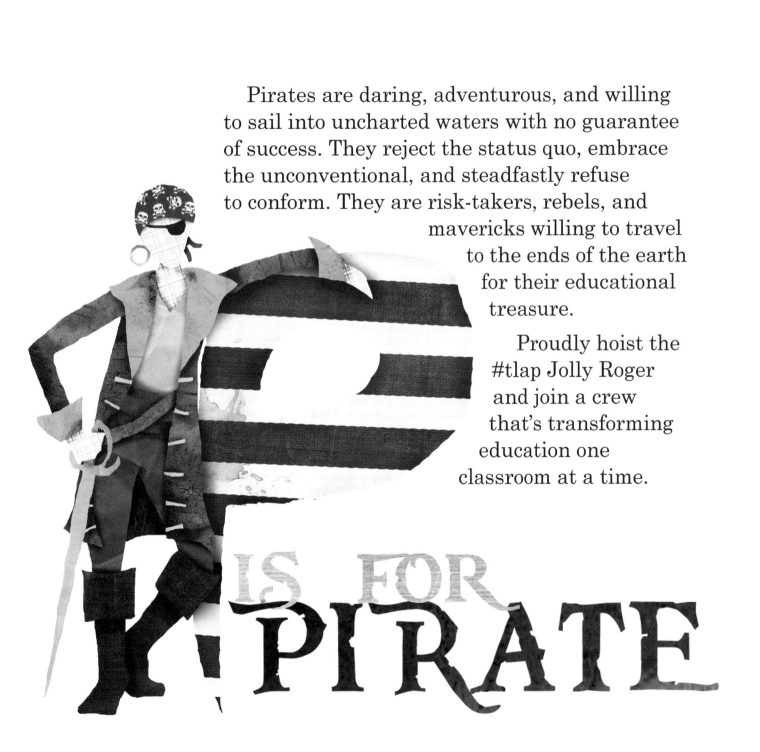

Pirates are daring, adventurous, and willing to sail into uncharted waters with no guarantee of success. They reject the status quo, embrace the unconventional, and steadfastly refuse to conform. They are risk-takers, rebels, and mavericks willing to travel to the ends of the earth for their educational treasure.

Proudly hoist the #tlap Jolly Roger and join a crew that's transforming education one classroom at a time.

IS FOR PIRATE

Everything matters. Are the lights on or off? What's written on the board? What song is playing? Should kids work in groups of two or three? Powerful lessons are the culmination of hundreds of presentational decisions. They can be haphazardly thrown together to create a threadbare blanket of boredom, or they can be intentionally woven into a beautiful rich quilt of engagement.

It all depends on how *you* stitch it.

Q is for QUILT

"Try to be a rainbow in someone's cloud."
~Maya Angelou

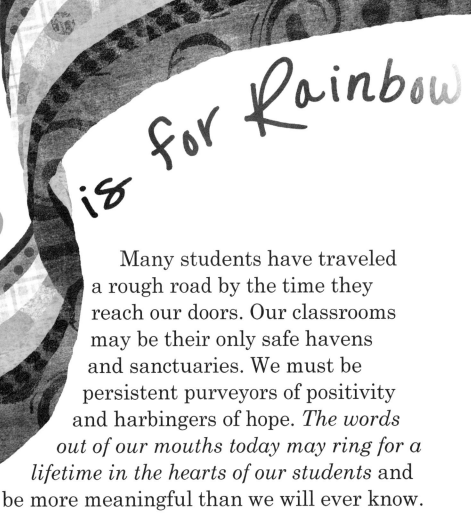

R is for Rainbow

Many students have traveled a rough road by the time they reach our doors. Our classrooms may be their only safe havens and sanctuaries. We must be persistent purveyors of positivity and harbingers of hope. *The words out of our mouths today may ring for a lifetime in the hearts of our students* and be more meaningful than we will ever know.

If you want to build a huge snowball, you can't pick up all the snow at once; it would just fall apart. You start small, pack it tight, and roll it slowly downhill. Snow sticks, and the snowball gains momentum as it grows.

You can't change a school's culture all at once, either. Change isn't something you just announce from the podium. Start small, build your crew, and above all...

is for

GET ROLLING.

snowball

is for **TAPIr**

The lions, tigers, bears, and monkeys draw most of the buzz at the zoo. Away from the crowds, dwelling in relative anonymity, reside equally significant and truly fascinating animals. They're the underdogs, the square pegs trying to fit into round holes, and those marching to the beat of a different drummer.

Here's to the tapirs of our schools—both students and adults. We are richer because of them.

U is for UN

Unwavering in our commitment.

Unleashed in our creativity.

Uncommon in our methods.

Unbroken in our spirit.

Unmatched in our effort.

Uninhibited in our passion.

Unabashed in our enthusiasm.

Uncompromising in the pursuit of excellence.

We need a lot more of this kind of "UN" in education.
(Don't forget to put the F in front of it, too!)

V is for velcro

Mnemonics

and

scaffolds

and

hooks,

oh my!

Great teachers possess treasure chests stocked with strategies and ideas to make sure learning sticks. Students need to engage with content in meaningful ways, so put handles on your material to make it easy for them to pick up!

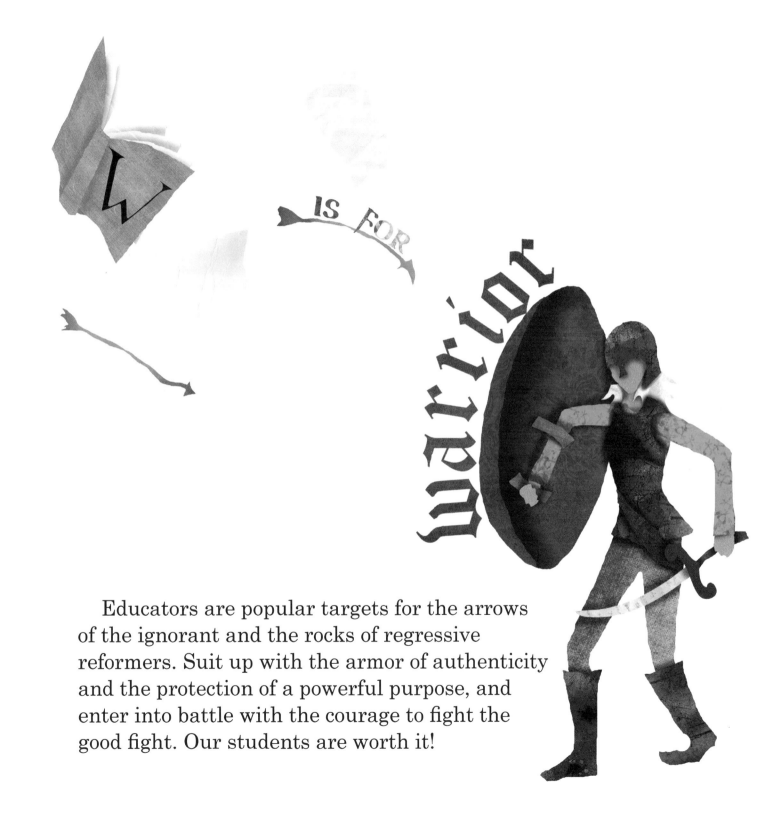

W IS FOR warrior

Educators are popular targets for the arrows of the ignorant and the rocks of regressive reformers. Suit up with the armor of authenticity and the protection of a powerful purpose, and enter into battle with the courage to fight the good fight. Our students are worth it!

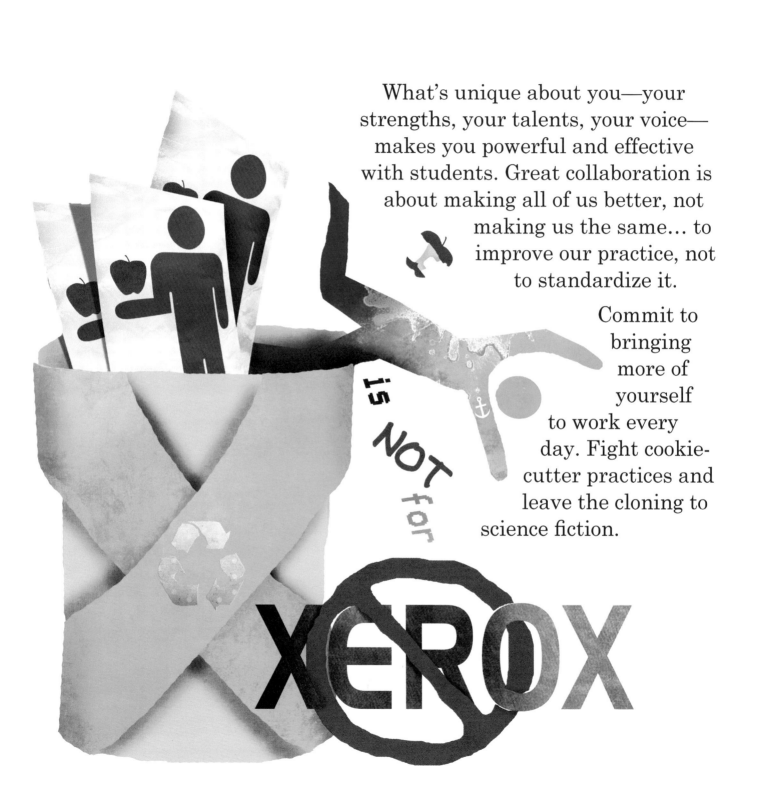

What's unique about you—your strengths, your talents, your voice—makes you powerful and effective with students. Great collaboration is about making all of us better, not making us the same... to improve our practice, not to standardize it.

Commit to bringing more of yourself to work every day. Fight cookie-cutter practices and leave the cloning to science fiction.

is NOT for

XEROX

If we don't tell our story, someone else will. We need to shape the message, create the agenda, and do more to toot our own horns. Relentlessly pitch and promote the positive things that happen daily on our campuses. **Shout** it from the mountaintop.

Marketing, salesmanship, and the art of persuasion are all proper tools in our toolbox. We are all in the P.R. department for education, our classes, and our kids.

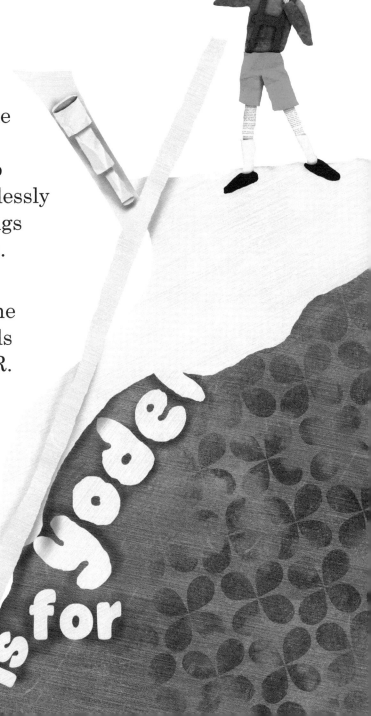

is for yodel

ZERØ
kids we can't reach.

ZERØ
lives that can't
be touched.

ZERØ
obstacles that
can't be overcome.

Z is for Ø

What we do is too important...
ZERO
Excuses!

Lead, Learn, and Teach
Like a Pirate!

More ABC's for Teaching Like a Pirate

WE HOPE you love the ideas we've shared, but we know that collaboration makes for a better education—and in this case an even better book. That's why we asked educators from across the country (and around the world) to share their thoughts on the ABC's of teaching like a pirate. From the many excellent responses we received from top-notch teachers and administrators, we pulled the best ideas to share with you.

ENJOY!

is also for...

Activism: Because education, our passions, and our students are worth the battle. Greg Curran @innov8reduc8r

And: The most powerful gift you can give your students is for them to have a love for learning *and* school. Be sure kids are learning *and* having fun at the same time; you'll be amazed at the difference it makes. Ryan McLane @mclane_ryan

is also for...

Banner: Carry a banner for students and the profession. Be a positive ambassador. Jimmy Casas @casas_Jimmy and Joy Kelly @joykelly05

Bliss: One of the most critical components of teaching is helping students find their passion—their bliss. Don Wettrick @DonWettrick

Box: Don't just think outside of it... annihilate it! Stephanie Frosch @Steph_Frosch

is also for...

Cape: It is undeniable... teachers are superheroes. Don your cape, harness your powers, take flight, and change lives each day. Barb Montfort @barb_montfort

Chain: We need to forge relationships with one another and with our students in order to be strong. You can't make a chain with only one link. Rhonda and Joe Corippo @rhondacorippo @jcorippo

is also for...

Deck: The all-hands-on-deck approach is crucial if we are to meet the needs of all learners. Parents, community members, teachers, and administrators must be vested and connected to ensure all students grow and can have a positive impact on the world. **Brad Currie @bradmcurrie**

Deejay: A great deejay knows that, when the dance floor is empty, it's time to change the song. The same principle works in the classroom. If kids are not engaged, you can hope for different kids, or you can change your lesson to engage the kids you have. **Joe Clark @DrJoeClark**

Detective: Sometimes educators need to be detectives to learn more about their students. We may have to investigate and look beneath the surface to discover their hearts and personalities.
Andrea Stringer @stringer_andrea

Drummer: Don't be afraid to march to the beat of your own drum. Mix it up and do things differently. Encourage your students to march to their own beat as well. If they have a different way to show their learning, let them! **Mickie Mueller @mickie_mueller**

is also for...

Echo: For some, an echo is all you hear if you never share your ideas with anyone. For others, the sound of the echo is a beacon, the siren's call that tells you it is time to initiate action. It is a signal that the time is right to share, to invite others in, to solicit feedback. Be brave and listen for voices other than your own. **Michael J. Podraza @ EGHSPrinciplRI**

Embark: We always need to be ready to embark on a new voyage whether it is the beginning of a new school year, a new semester, or even a new day. Every day is an adventure in teaching. **Lisa Milstead @LisaMilstead**

Energy: Every school has its own energy. It can pull you in or make you want to leave. Every interaction creates the energy in your school. How will you contribute to it? **Joe Sanfelippo @Joesanfelippofc**

is also for...

Flip: Flipping our mindsets means putting the introductory information into the individual spaces so we can put the deep thinking, further explanations, and connections into the shared space. How can we make the most effective use of our time together with a collaborative group of great students and a professional teacher in the same room? Flipping gets us started. **Jason Bretzmann @jbretzmann**

Freak: Let your freak flag fly! Don't be shy about what makes you uniquely *you*. Own it! **Amy Presley @STLinOK**

is also for...

Gamification: The technique of using the most motivational aspects of games in a non-game setting like our classrooms allows students to participate in challenge-based learning and various quests. Jumping into an *immersive* and *gamified* learning environment increases student engagement and achievement. **Michael Matera @MrMatera**

Genius: Students are led to find their inner genius when they are allowed to explore their own passions in the classroom. Allow them to seek answers, solve problems, and be innovative. **#geniushour Chris Kesler @iamkesler**

Giraffe: Stick your neck out, people! Giraffes know that their best source of nutrition is out of reach to others. What great classroom adventure awaits in the creativity just beyond the reach of mediocrity? Reach for it! **Christy Cate @christycate**

is also for...

Ham: When teachers seek their inner ham, they can connect with students in humanizing, humorous ways. **Lynne Perednia @Perednia**

Haven: Our goal as educators is to create a safe haven for children where they are comfortable taking risks with their learning, confident in their surroundings, and feel loved and secure. **Tony Sinanis @TonySinanis**

Helm: Rather than just complain about the lack of vision or the wrong course being charted, innovative educators seize the helm in order to make change happen. **John Berray @JohnBerray**

Hunger: Though some may consider teachers to be experts, our true expertise lies in our hunger and our willingness to pursue what we don't know. Our job is to live out that hunger in front of our students. **Steve Wyborney @SteveWyborney**

is also for...

Ice: While ice can be chilling, ice is also invigorating, refreshing, and provides comfort in times of hot stress. Keep the ice around. You never know when you'll need to provide comfort and relief! **Jay Eitner @iSuperEit**

Inchworm: Educators must take steps forward, no matter how small, in order to learn and grow. Every step seems small, but when taken consistently, one can look back and see great progress. **Jennifer Hogan @Jennifer_Hogan**

Ink: Ready. Set. Make your mark! Teaching is the opportunity to make a difference in the life of a child. Likewise, students get the chance to discover their potential and path... they have empty pages ready to be written. **Jennifer Diszler @Jenniferdiz**

Island: An island doesn't have to mean isolation. It is surrounded by the ocean waves, lapping on the shores, shifting the sand. The #tlap community is like those waves—constantly offering a push or a nudge when needed as well as support for teachers who may feel isolated. **Lori London @SciTeach7Davis**

is also for...

Journey: The destination we seek as educators is important, but perhaps not as important as the journey we take with students to get there. Brett Murray @sciology

Jump: Jump out of your comfort zone and try something new. Make your teaching unexpected today. Laura Farmer @laurabethfarmer

is also for...

Kakooma: Games engage kids to practice skills and motivate students in ways that worksheets never will. Any game with a little competition and teamwork will bring out the best in most kids. Mary Kienstra @beebeKienstra

Kibbutz: A kibbutz is a communal settlement, typically a farm. Make your classroom a kibbutz! You're not planting crops or milking cows, but the best classroom is one that has a communal feeling where the students and teacher work together to achieve a common goal. Matt Barry @MrBarry628

Kick: We all need support from time to time—sometimes with a swift kick and other times with a gentle nudge. Know when you need which, and find the right person to do it. #BrainPowered LaVonna Roth @LaVonnaRoth

Kite: Young minds should soar high and free while we keep a thin, but secure hold on them, guiding gently so they don't crash. Kathleen Kryza @kathleenkryza

is also for...

Lighthouse: Educators are beacons of bright lights for students, helping them navigate the sea of learning. Sydney Musslewhite @smussle

Lion: Teachers must *ROAR* to have their voices heard to challenge the status quo and mediocrity. They must be leaders, unafraid to stand out from the crowd, to take the path less traveled, and to be innovators. Teachers are the voice of education and must be uncompromising champions of all students. Roar for all to hear! Ben Brazeau @braz74

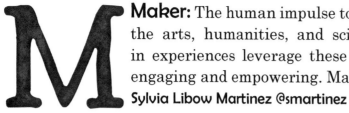

Maker: The human impulse to create and make sense of the world drives the arts, humanities, and sciences to new heights. Hands-on, heads-in experiences leverage these impulses into authentic learning that is engaging and empowering. Making real things makes things real.
Sylvia Libow Martinez @smartinez

is also for...

Mirror: Students and teachers need opportunities to reflect... on their learning, practices, strengths, and needs. Build in time to look in the mirror. Amy Illingworth @AmyLIllingworth

Myth: Each of us brings preconceived notions to our craft that prevent us from effectively growing as pedagogues. It's our duty to see the truth in education and to elevate students to their own greatness.
Starr Sackstein @mssackstein

Navigate: We provide the tools and skills students need to navigate a successful education, but we should let them steer their own ship.
Brandi Murray @TechChique

Ninety-nine: Never think that anything is 100% complete—you can always do better. You can always make the best better.
Craig Kemp @mrkempnz

is also for...

Now: Don't wait to make your classroom amazing... do it *now*!
Ashlyn Burgess (Pirate daughter, age 11)

is also for...

Open: An open teacher welcomes the class at the door and shares her passions and knowledge with her students, while being open to grow from change and others' ideas. **Melany Wellnitz @melwellnitz**

Origami: Some people might see a simple piece of paper. But someone practiced in origami sees so much more: the paper's potential. With folds and imagination, this simple piece of paper becomes a beautiful creation. In a similar way, a passionate teacher can create something amazing and memorable out of a simple lesson. Don't be fooled when you encounter an ordinary lesson. With imagination and vision, it can become a masterpiece. **Julie Nilsson Smith @julnilsmith**

Owning it: Teaching is not just what we do... teaching is what we are! Let's own it—in our classrooms, at our schools, and throughout our communities. **Alex Kajitani @AlexKajitani**

is also for...

Pique: Pique the spirit of curiosity and light the fire of learning for students. **Dwight Stevenson @dwsteven**

Prosperity: A classroom is meant to be the land of prosperity, from the first welcome of the first day until the good-byes of the last. It is the wealth of knowledge and experience collected by the learners within that awakens the soul to its quest to learn. **Kimberly Hurd Horst @khurdhorst**

Punk Rock Teaching: The reason there were so many punk bands was that no one expected to hear a flawless musician. People filled concert halls because of passion and an idea. Do you have passion and an idea? Then get going! Quit waiting until your idea or teaching is perfect. **David Theriault @davidtedu**

is also for...

Quirks: Once labeled weird or crazy, pirate teachers find that their quirks are exactly what helps them build rapport with their students. Instead of hiding them, using quirkiness to engage students makes a pirate really tick. **Sandy Otto @sandyrotto**

QWERTY: Sometimes you have to be willing to change and innovate to improve. Don't just use outdated ideas; blaze your own path.
Hayden Burgess (Pirate son, age 13)

is also for...

Reef: Innovation, creativity, and some of the other most beautiful parts of being an educator lie under the surface and are sometimes difficult to reach. **Andrea Kornowski @andreakornowski**

Return: Every day, we are given grace by those who know us best and need us the most. Do not forget to return that grace and offer it to others.
Eric Chagala @drchagala

Rigging: Relationships are the rigging that gives support and structure to a community of learners. **Sandy King @sandeeteach**

is also for...

Second chances: All children deserve second chances. Don't allow their past decisions or reputations to define how you are going to treat them.
Todd Nesloney @TechNinjaTodd

Service: Educators are in the service business; they put their students' needs first. Being of service to others is probably the only way to become truly fulfilled. **Hal Roberts @HalLRoberts**

Sparkle: Students should see a sparkle when they look in your eyes. Your love of teaching and learning is palpable and contagious.
Jamie Palmer @jamiepa79

Sutler: When innovating teaching practices, teachers must be willing to communicate their rationale to parents, other teachers, and students. Essentially, teachers must get others to buy into the value of doing things differently. **Alice Keeler @alicekeeler**

is also for...

Tinkering: Give your students chances to create, play, make mistakes, and try again. **Sean Farnum @MagicPantsJones**

Toolbox: Teachers have so many tools in their toolboxes. Some are shiny and new, and others are old, but tried and true. Success is not found in the tool itself, but rather in a teacher's creative way to use the tool to make connections with students and their interests. **JoAnn Fox @AppEducationFox**

Turbulence: When we veer from the well-worn path, the ride may get a bit bumpy. This turbulence is just a reminder that we are learning and growing. **David Culberhouse @dculberhouse**

is also for...

Unicorn: We should always encourage students to believe and imagine, and then let them decide where the truth lies. Perhaps it's with a horse with a pointy horn. **Barry Saide @barrykid1**

Unshakeable: Don't let the everyday hassles of teaching throw you off your game! Stay focused on your vision, and surround yourself with passionate educators. Continually look for creative ways to tap into your inner motivation. Your enthusiasm for teaching will become contagious and unshakeable. **Angela Watson @Angela_Watson**

is also for...

VavaVOOM: Go hard or go home every day! Kick it up a notch and amplify each lesson to the next level. **Beth Houf @BethHouf**

Volume: Don't be afraid to turn it up to an 11! **Melissa Milner @teach1991**

is also for...

Weird: The silly, strange, goofy, and sideways will always be more engaging than the beige, boring, normal, and status quo.
Doug Robertson @TheWeirdTeacher

Why: Kids are entitled, if not compelled, to ask "Why?" Why do we have to learn this? Why am I here? When teachers focus on the "why" it creates purpose. *Why* is about learning and life.
Scott Bedley and Tim Bedley @BedleyBros

Wingman: In the Air Force, the wingman flies beside or behind the pilot, providing protection and support. As educators, we are wingmen for our students, providing support and encouragement as we allow them to take flight and lead their own learning. **Cynthia Smith-Ough @SmithOugh**

is also for...

X-factor: That certain, unexplained something that happens during a lesson that makes learning amazing! **Scott Rocco @ScottRRocco**

X-ray: Be transparent. Be real. Be who you are. See the inside of yourself and others... see what's really going on. **Wendy Claussen @kiddielitprof**

Xenophile: Look for the outliers and make them part of your community.
Christine Esposito @espolearns

Yearning: Leave your students wanting to learn more so that they yearn to seek that knowledge for themselves. **Ashley Graville @PrimaryTeachNC**

Yoga: Yoga involves gentle movements, graceful stretching, and multiple positions to enhance peace of mind, strength of body, and serenity. The many layers of yoga help us live healthy lives. Learning is much the same. Educators and students alike move through the layers of learning to feel strong, create balance, find peace, and *grow!*

"The most important pieces of equipment you need for doing yoga are your body and your mind." ~Rodney Yee .... The same holds true for *learning.* **Kathy Perret @KathyPerret**

Yo-Yo: *La enseñanza puede tener sus altos y sus bajos. Practicamos los trucos para conectar e inspirar a nuestros estudiantes.* [Teaching can have its ups and downs. We practice the tricks to hook and inspire our students.] **Yau-Jau Ku @yaujauku**

is also for...

is also for...

Zen: Simplify, reduce, and subtract. Be present in the moment to find the essence of your lesson. Accepting what is leads to learning and peace. **Danny Tricarico @TheZenTeacher**

Zephyr: Zephyr is a light wind or west wind. Think about taking advantage of the teachable moment to provide amazing experiences, letting the students lead the way. Go where the zephyr takes you. **Jay Billy @JayBilly2**

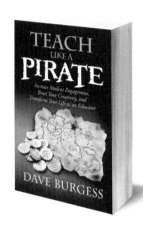

Teach Like a PIRATE
Increase Student Engagement, Boost Your Creativity, and Transform Your Life as an Educator

By Dave Burgess

Teach Like a PIRATE is the *New York Times* best-selling book that has sparked a worldwide educational revolution. It is part inspirational manifesto that ignites passion for the profession and part practical road map filled with dynamic strategies to dramatically increase student engagement. Translated into four languages, its message resonates with educators who want to design outrageously creative lessons and transform school into a life-changing experience for students.

Pure Genius
Building a Culture of Innovation and Taking 20% Time to the Next Level

By Don Wettrick (@DonWettrick)

For far too long, schools have been bastions of boredom, killers of creativity, and way too comfortable with compliance and conformity. In *Pure Genius*, Don Wettrick explains how collaboration—with experts, students, and other educators—can help you create interesting, and even life-changing opportunities for learning. Wettrick's book inspires and equips educators with a systematic blueprint for teaching innovation in *any* school.

Coming in 2015

Learn Like a PIRATE

By Paul Solarz (@PaulSolarz)

Today's job market demands that students be prepared to take responsibility for their lives and careers. We do them a disservice if we teach them how to earn passing grades without equipping them to take charge of their education. In *Learn Like a Pirate*, Paul Solarz explains how to design classroom experiences that encourage students to take risks and explore their passions in a stimulating, motivating, and supportive environment where improvement, rather than grades, is the focus. Discover how student-led classrooms help students thrive and develop into self-directed, confident citizens who are capable of making smart, responsible decisions, all on their own.

Ditch that Textbook

By Matt Miller (@jmattmiller)

Textbooks are symbols of centuries of old education. They're often outdated as soon as they hit students' desks. Acting "by the textbook" implies compliance and a lack of creativity. It's time to ditch those textbooks—and those textbook assumptions about learning! In *Ditch that Textbook*, teacher and blogger Matt Miller encourages educators to throw out meaningless, pedestrian teaching and learning practices. It empowers them to evolve and improve on old, standard teaching methods. *Ditch that Textbook* is a support system, toolbox, and manifesto to help educators free their teaching and revolutionize their classrooms.

About the Authors

Dave and Shelley Burgess are the co-owners of Dave Burgess Consulting, Inc., which specializes in transforming education through professional development programs and publishing.

Dave is the *New York Times* best-selling author of *Teach Like a PIRATE: Increase Student Engagement, Boost Your Creativity, and Transform Your Life as an Educator*. He is a highly sought-after professional development speaker well known for his outrageously energetic and creative style. His programs not only inspire and motivate educators but also provide practical strategies to dramatically improve instruction and student engagement. He has been an award-winning teacher for over seventeen years and was the Academy of Education Arts and Sciences BAMMY recipient for Secondary School Teacher of the Year in 2014.

Shelley has served twenty years as an award-winning teacher, principal, Director of Student Achievement, and most recently, Assistant Superintendent of Educational Leadership. She has led major reform initiatives that resulted in significant improvements in teaching and learning at both the school and district level. Her highly respected work has focused on building the leadership capacity of both administrators and teachers through coaching, collaboration, and building a positive culture of change. Shelley now works as a full-time partner in Dave Burgess Consulting, Inc.

Dave and Shelley live in San Diego, California, with their amazing children, Hayden and Ashlyn, two spunky dogs, Aspen and Coco, a bearded dragon lizard, three aquariums of fish, and their unflappable cat, Raven, who tolerates them all.

Connect with Dave and Shelley on Twitter (@burgessdave and @burgess_shelley) and join the #tlap chats. Learn more at DaveBurgessConsulting.com.

CPSIA information can be obtained
at www.ICGtesting.com
Printed in the USA
BVIC02n0950220815
414003BV00018B/137